I Think I Might

A Guide to Spotting the Signs and Symptoms and Living with Autism

Table of Contents

Introduction

As someone who has worked with both autistic adults and children for the majority of my career, I have experienced an amazing inside look into the lives of many of individuals who suffer from the condition.

Something that I find fascinating about the condition is the amount of people that have gone undiagnosed for years, only to find as an adult they suffer from some of the symptoms associated with the condition, and going to their doctor about an issue and finding out almost by chance they are autistic.

It seems to be one of only a few illnesses that have this characteristic.

I believe this is largely due to the huge swings in severity of symptoms between individuals. One positive thing I now notice however, is that autism is much more widely discussed and publicized than it's ever been, giving more people an opportunity to recognize their symptoms and finally get answers to problems that can cause a huge amount of frustration in day to day living.

This book is the culmination of four years research, talking to people and children who suffer with autism, many of whom went undiagnosed for some time due to having a high functioning autistic condition such as Asperger's .

In my research I have noticed very similar frustrations in a lot of people, and these are things I have tried to discuss in this book and some of the strategies we have used to eliminate these things.

This book contains everything from the symptoms and recognizing you or a loved one had autism, to both medical interventions and things you can do at home to alleviate the issues caused.

The books aims to delve deeper into pressure people with autism face such as awkwardness in social situations or unexplained repetitive behaviors, and help you put into place practical techniques that will help control such activities.

Chapter 1 - What is Autism- the Basics

We don't often think about adults having conditions like autism, this is because it is mainly publicized as a childhood condition. When we see autism news in the media, it is usually correlated with children.

What happens when those children grow up?

In addition to that, not all autistic adults were diagnosed as children. It is true that there has been a swell of diagnosis as of late, but sometimes the disorder isn't properly diagnosed, is misdiagnosed, or is missed completely. Therefore, there are more and more adults that have the condition that have never been formally diagnosed.

Autism is now much more widely talked about and seen on TV and in the media, which is alerting more people to the possibility of the condition being present either for themselves or for friends and family members, but because it is only recently Autism in adults has become more recognized, there seems to be less advice readily available than there is for children suffering with the same condition.

33% of all diagnosed cases of autism are present in adults. Most of these are diagnosed as children. Many of these adults have a very mild condition of autism such as Asperger's and are fully capable of living and working on their own with no outside help. Symptoms for these people can be fleeting or minimal or have flare ups when provoked by stressful situations. However, some adults who have a low functioning autistic condition need extra support or care and some require 24 hour care or supervised living.

That being said, there are so many different factors and variants in the autistic spectrum. Many adults with high functioning autism are incredibly successful, I have met many adults with autism who have ran their own businesses or worked in very scientific roles. They still have certain difficulties that they have to find coping mechanisms for, such as relating to other individuals but they have got their condition to a level of control that allows them to live relatively normally, and only now and again being pushed out of their comfort zone.

At its heart, autism is a neurodevelopmental disorder. It normally appears during infancy or during childhood. There is no "cure" and it does not go into "remission". Through various treatments, more overt symptoms can become less explicit when in adulthood. These symptoms generally come in a triad: social interaction, hindrances in communication, and restricted interests/repetitive behaviors.

These symptoms can lead to further secondary symptoms, such as frustration or depression, but this is not the case in every individual, and throughout my work this is the most important thing I have learnt. Every single case is individual, their symptoms have differing levels of severity, their attitudes towards what will work for them differ, which is why I have tried to add as many treatment options and techniques as possible to this book, so you can work out what is best for you and what would work for you as an individual.

Having worked with children in the past, attaining a degree in education with courses in alternative education, and having family members that are autistic, I am confident in saying that with a little extra care and effective treatments, high functioning autism can be handled well. Yes, it can at times take perseverance, but the results are absolutely worth it.

If you are an adult or a young adult who may be considering the fact that he or she has autism, chances are that if you have autism, you have a higher functioning form of the disorder which could have been missed in childhood. This is not uncommon, and it is not something you need to worry about, there is help available, and often the stress caused by worrying can actually enhance the symptoms associated with the condition.

High functioning autism is sometimes also referred to as Asperger's syndrome. While these two disorders are similar, they are not necessarily the same.

High functioning autism is at the far end of the autistic spectrum. Symptoms are less severe. People with higher functioning autism usually have an average or above-average intelligence. These symptoms that linger in adulthood are manageable with a little practice and perseverance.

What are the differences between Autism and Asperger's Syndrome?

Asperger's syndrome and High-functioning Autism are both part of the condition generally termed the 'Autistic Spectrum'.

The primary difference between the two conditions is generally thought to be concerning language development. People with Asperger's syndrome will not have displayed a marked delay in language development when younger. Delayed language development at a very young age is primarily related to Autism.

For most cases, the symptoms and treatment can be considered the same although slight differences in diagnosis do exist.

1) The idea that Asperger's syndrome is autism without any additional learning difficulties is often helpful in the early stages of diagnosis as it is fairly easy to differentiate. There are unusual cases where a person could present the symptoms of Asperger's syndrome and still have other learning difficulties. It is generally agreed that high-functioning autism cannot occur in a person with an IQ below 65.

2) Recent developments have led us to the understanding that Asperger's syndrome can only

occur when there are extra difficulties with basic motor skills. It is common to find that children with Asperger's syndrome also exhibit poor co-ordination and have difficulty with motor skills. It should be noted however that many children with high-level autism will also exhibit these problem area.

3) Language development in high-functioning autism is usually slow but Asperger's syndrome shows no indication of this. A key point in the diagnosis of Asperger's syndrome states that language development must be normal. Children with high-functioning autism usually develop language skills much later than expected. As diagnosis in children often happens when they reach an older stage it is often difficult to rely on parents to identify problems with language development in the earlier years before diagnosis.

4) Asperger's syndrome can usually not be determined until the child has at least reached school age. Often, a child who has been diagnosed with high-functioning autism in early years is reclassified to Asperger's syndrome after they have started school. This is usually credited with the fact that social skills, or deficits in this area, may not be obvious until the child spends a lot of time in social interaction with others of a similar age.

To try to generalize, both high-functioning autism and Asperger's syndrome are likely to be of higher level intelligence and exhibit traits common to both conditions. It is still debatable as to the need for two different diagnoses as they both appear very similar and the treatment is often identical.

Although it is often unhelpful and worrying to be presented with a diagnosis which is not clearly defined it is important to remember that the basic symptoms of both conditions are mainly the same.

This means that the treatments, approaches and therapy methods are often also the same.

At all times it is important to remember that every person with either autism or Asperger's syndrome is different and unique with their own set of abilities and skills.

If your child has recently been diagnosed with either condition or you yourself have it is often worthwhile asking what criteria were used for the diagnosis. This can help you create a treatment plan that is individual to your circumstances and specific symptoms.

How did I get Autism or Asperger's Syndrome?

Autism can be genetic; studies have shown it can run in families. However, the direct cause is unknown. Scientists are unaware of the underlying causes other than genetics.

There is still much research to be done on this and many studies are underway exploring the effect of many factors on autism such as environmental factors or underlying medical conditions.

The continual challenge faced in the determination of the cause or causes underlining the development of autism is due to the lack of one sole cause. Several factors have been researched and linked to the development of autism without any one being attributed to being the sole factor.

Obesity during pregnancy along with diabetes have been attributed in some part to increasing the risk of autism although it is clear that most mothers were not obese during pregnancy nor were they diabetic.

This shows that this cannot be the sole cause of autism in children but can only be attributed to increasing the risk. Studies have shown that obesity and diabetes during pregnancy might have a factor on the development of the child's brain.

Everything inside our body involves biochemistry. Cells are constantly involved in chemical reactions with both the building and breaking down of substances during our metabolism within our body. Anything that can interrupt this process could cause problems.

Genes can cause problems, so can environmental factors. Toxins in the body can affect our metabolic actions. Sometimes the changes are too minute for our bodies to realize, but they are happening never the less. This means that both environmental factors as well as genetic factors could affect health during pregnancy. Opinion has developed that it may be possible for these factors, such as genetic and environmental factors, to be passed on to the fetus.

This does not in itself cause autism but may have an impact of the development of the child in the early years. Preventing these complications may not be the single way of preventing autism but they give a good foundation for the developing child.

Studies have shown that families that have autism in their genetic lines also have family members with higher levels of: Anxiety, Depression, Obsessive-compulsive disorder, Tourette's syndrome (the most severe tic disorder, characterized by both physical and vocal tics), Transient tic disorder (the presence of a tic(s) that appear for at least a month but no longer than a year), Chronic physical or vocal tic disorder (unlike transient tics, these last for more than a year with the stipulation that symptoms appear before the age of 18).

These studies suggest that there is some type of relationship with these different mental disorders and processes of the brain which also have a large part to play in autism.

Autism spectrum disorders have a tendency of co-occurring with other diseases or disorders. The most common is epilepsy or seizure disorder. Some other examples are tuberous sclerosis, various types of learning disabilities, anxiety disorders, attention deficit hyperactivity disorder, obsessive compulsive disorder and sensory processing disorder.

One thing that is recognized is that the symptoms of high functioning autism or Asperger's are often brought about by stressful situations or situations that would be uncomfortable for the individual.

As an example of this, a sufferer who is naturally uncomfortable in social situations may notice their condition and symptoms worsening when put in a situation where they have to socialize.

I worked with one young man who when you spoke with him one on one was perfectly in control of his emotions, but when he attended an event for autistic teenagers, his symptoms instantly worsened, he became unable to make eye contact with anyone in the room, and found that he was segregating himself from the rest of the guests.

Self-alienation is one of the most common forms of self-preservation I have seen when working with autistic people, and that in itself can be detrimental to living a normal life, as it makes it difficult to make and forge relationships.

Specific Challenges that Adults with Autism Face

I cannot pinpoint every single challenge that you may currently face as an adult with autism or as someone whom suspects they may have autism.

Every person (adult and child) with autism is a unique individual and thus, each faces a different struggle. However, generally speaking, adults with autism normally face at least one of these certain difficulties:

- Persistent Troubles with Social Communication & Social Interactions

- Restricted/Repetitive Patterns (in terms of behavior, activities, and interests)

- Feelings of Frustration when someone has a differing opinion

- Sense of unease when something changes with regular patterns.

Some adults will struggle with day to day living but not realize why. Being diagnosed with autism can explain some of these struggles.

Ask yourself, do you struggle with more than one of these things?

1) Moving from school to school or from job to job

2) Being uncomfortable with change

3) Keeping or finding a job

4) Maintaining relationships

5) Enjoyment of leisure time due to anxiety

6) Over-planning small things such as trips, shopping or the food you eat

7) A sense of awkwardness when faced with new people or situations

8) Starting friendships

9) Becoming easily frustrated or anxious if things do not go quite to plan

These are all possible problems that a person with autism could face.

Do you have friends or relatives that struggle maintaining healthy relationships with you? They may be trying hard but just don't know how to connect with you and vice versa. Finding a diagnosis of autism may help alleviate that tension because once you diagnose the problem, you can find the best solution for it. Chances are it is a communication issue or common issues such as changes or disagreements causing clashes between you and loved ones, and when I have worked with families, I have found that it can be just as frustrating for family members, trying to connect with someone who has the condition.

It is often the case that adults with autism often struggle to do the day to day tasks that other people may take for granted. The list above gives just the main areas of problem that can cause disruption to daily life.

Because an adult with autism reacts differently to different situations they can often face a life of exclusion from peer groups or even family members, and even prejudice and/or bullying.

These factors often magnify the reactions to problematic situations, often causing depression, anxiety or other secondary symptoms that come with the issues autism sufferers can face due to their communication issues.

Understanding the causes of these problems is often just the first step needed to resolving them. Understanding is often key, but it is not only about educating autism sufferers about their condition and how to deal with it, often it is about educating peers and loved ones of how to deal with certain situations in a way that won't cause any unnecessary tension.

So when you come to the home treatment section of this book, you will find we have included a number of exercises that involve a friend or a family member helping out. This includes them in your struggle and helps them understand how your mind works.

Autism Symptoms-What to Look For.

Symptoms of Autism can vary hugely from person to person.

There are some very subtle signs of autism such as verbal signs, difficulties with social interactions, difficulties in relationships, etc. where someone with autism could be simply considered "shy" to an outsider, and the extent of these symptoms vary depending on where on the autistic spectrum a condition would lie. For example, Asperger's syndrome would generally speaking carry a lower level of noticeable symptom.

The core symptoms of Autism and Asperger's can be similar but the severity of each symptom can vary quite a bit.

The categories are as follows:

1) Limited interests in activities or fascination with specific aspects of certain activities.

2) Relationships with other people and social interactions can be strained.

3) Communication (both verbal and nonverbal) can be affected, often this will manifest in the form of being unable to touch another person or make eye contact.

All three categories affect both children and adults who have autism. Usually they are more noticeable in children who are diagnosed with the condition, simply because they were noticeable enough to be diagnosed as a child. A person who has managed to conceal such symptoms until adulthood, usually will have symptoms which display much less severity.

In the next few chapters I have broken these symptoms down even further, so we can take a look at some specifics so that you can better evaluate your specific situation.

This will really help you to look at putting together a treatment plan which is not only suitable for you, but designed to your specific needs and the issues you personally face.

Chapter 2 - Repetitive Behaviors & Limited Interests in Activities

This covers quite a range of interests. However the most common symptoms that fit under this category are:

Focusing Heavily on Certain Pieces of an Object.

This is often called restricted behavior.

This is more prevalent in younger children but can pop up in the normal, everyday behaviors of adults as well, often as a subconscious activity.

In children, the tendency is to focus on certain parts of toys instead of playing with the entire toy. For example, if he has a toy plane, he may just focus on the propeller instead of playing with the whole plane.

I have seen this in adults in work situations, one of the ladies I worked with in the past was given a project to do for her job, she was given a week to complete the project which involved three tasks. She became so focused on the first task, almost to a level of obsession, that she spent six days of her seven day deadline on it.

Concentration

Concentrating on certain topics for an unusually long amount of time, despite what is going on around. This is another form of restricted behavior.

This is seen more with older children and adults and is another version of the previous symptom.

Examples of this behavior would include a fascination and heightened emphasis on items and activities like video games, license plates, trading cards, movies or music, and showing a lack of interest in other activities.

This can be harder to pinpoint since teenagers and adults will often focus on something as a hobby. However, pay special attention to how much devotion you give to these things, and your openness to explore new things outside of the given interest.

The Necessity for Routine

Often called ritualistic behavior.

This is a tendency that pops up with both young children and adults.

In children who have autism, there may be an unnecessary devotion to a specific routine: eating dinner in the same order every night, going the same route to a specific destination, putting on clothes in the same order, etc.

As an adult, this is more difficult to pinpoint if you have a particularly hectic schedule or routine, and the issue is that most adults adhere to some kind of routine or timetable within their daily lives so it can be an easy symptom to miss. However, if you feel unusually uneasy when your routine varies or when something unexpectedly changes, it could be a good indicator of this particular symptom causing issues for you.

Repetitive Behavior

There are various forms of repetitive behaviors including – but not restricted to :

1) Stereotypy (repetitive movements like body rocking)

2) Compulsive behavior (intentional follow through of rules that he regulates like positioning objects in certain arrangements)

3) Self-injury (compulsive movements that can often harm like skin-picking, head-banging, and eye-poking). This behavior is more often seen in young children who are diagnosed with autism.

None of these repetitive behaviors seem to be specific to autism, which is one of the issues facing doctors when trying to diagnose the condition.

That being said, an elevated pattern of these behaviors and its severity seem to be characteristic of autism.

Some research has shown that repetitive behaviors develop early in autism. On average, children who developed autism showed four to eight symptoms of repetitive behavior at the age of twelve months compared with children who did not develop autism showing just one or two.

Examples of repetitive behavior in very young children include hand flapping, spinning and rocking. While experts agree that some repetitive behavior is required for general development the number of incidences in children who developed autism were greater.

Whereas in adults repetitive behaviors are often associated with more logical or practical tasks.

The suggestions are that due to these repetitive behavior trends, parents can often be the ideal point of first detection and intervention for children who may be sufferers of the condition.

Chapter 3 - Difficulty in Social Situations and Forming and Maintaining Relationships

This symptom is what really distinguishes autism from other conditions.

It is often the most noticeable and the most problematic condition. Often causing the most anxiety and stress to suffers than all of the other symptoms.

Those who have autism are found to lack intuition about social norms, interactions with others, and how to build relationships.

In children these inabilities become apparent as they interact (or don't interact) with the people around them.

As an adult with autism, the condition can come and go in certain circumstances or in situations where the sufferer is out of their usual comfort zone.

Symptoms related to social difficulties can include the following:

1)Difficulty looking people in the eye. This can cause extreme anxiety.

2) Difficulty touching people, sufferers may be uncomfortable with shaking hands or hugging.

3) Difficulty 'taking turns'. In children this could be when playing with toys, however, in adults the sufferer can miss conversational cues such as when someone finished speaking.

5) Often sufferers will find it difficult to pick up on others emotions, so may not realize when it is appropriate to act happy or sad.

6) Difficulty Defining and using the appropriate social norms.

7) Difficulty making new friends. Often making new friends involves new social situations and often this is something autism sufferers do not handle well. They would also find it extremely difficult to initiate a conversation. Children with the condition are often seen as "loners".

8) The ability to develop and maintain relationships is difficult. The struggle of beginning a relationship is one thing, but an autism sufferer can find it extremely difficult to develop an interaction into a friendship or romantic relationship and to maintain that bond. This is quite often to do with the fact that many autism sufferers have a problem with inflexibility and change. This can manifest in them becoming frustrated in situations where a person does not share the same opinion or desire to do something.

In Children you may notice they have problems building relationships with peers or other adults but they do form strong attachments to their primary caregivers, often becoming clingy or portraying evidence of separation anxiety, on the complete opposite end of the scale, some children will show an extreme lack of emotion as an autism sufferer, and will not show any concern when left in a room with strangers. This is the reason autism can be very difficult to diagnose properly as the same symptom can vary so much between different individuals.

Both children and adults will often not relate to new situations very well. They prefer the known and comfort of their own enclosed environment.

If you are reading this book because you are concerned you may have Autism, ask yourself these questions:

1)What types of relationships do you have with others?

2) How do you connect with other people? On an emotional level? On a social level? On a mental level? On a physical level?

3) How do you feel in social situations? Do you get overly anxious?

4) Are you often referred to as socially awkward or shy?

5) Do you have problems distinguishing what social norms are appropriate in various social situations?

6) Do you suffer from an intense feeling of loneliness despite preferring to spend time to yourself?

7) Do you find it difficult to connect with strangers to form friendships or other types of relationships?

8) Do you find it difficult to maintain friendships?

9) Is it hard to know what is expected of you in any situations involving others?

10) Are you uncomfortable moving into new situations?

11) Do you find yourself frustrated or anxious when your routine is forced to changed?

Chapter 4 - Communication Issues

Trouble communicating is another symptom of autism. This can be seen in toddlers, young children, adolescents, and adults who have autism.

When seen in young children and toddlers, this can be overt: they just don't develop enough natural speech to meet their needs.

In adults it is can often more of an inability to get a point across in a socially acceptable manner or without suffering anxiety which can cause stuttering.

The ability to communicate your needs verbally may not be an issue for you – as an adult. However, there are other forms of communication and understanding of communication that can be affected by the condition.

Think about your current behavior and try to answer these questions:

1) Do you have issues taking the steps to initiate a conversation?

2) Do you have difficulties trying to continue a conversation after it has started?

3) Do you find it difficult to understand ideas, concepts, thoughts, and perceptions through another person's perspective? An example of this would be the miscommunication of the use of humor and being too literal with humor.

4) Do you find yourself accidentally using reverse pronouns?

Now, think back to when you were a child and try to answer these questions (your parents might be more helpful in this matter):

1) Were you delayed in developing language techniques? (Note that boys often say their first words later than girls do.)

2) Did you have a repetitive use of language? An example would be latching onto a phrase or word and repeating it over and over again. This is called echolalia.

3) As an infant, it is also common to see a deficit in joint attention (the ability for two people to focus on the same thing. For example, if mom points to an object and the child follows those verbal cues – pointing, eye-gazing, or other verbal/nonverbal cues – and then returns his gaze to mom. The deficit comes from the infant consistently staring at mom's pointing hand instead of following it.

4) Children with autism also have difficulty with imaginative games like make-believe, playing house, and developing symbols into culture/language. Often their cognitive skills are very well developed, so their logical mind will function extremely well, but the creative side of the mind may not.

Establishing whether your condition was simply "missed" as a child, or whether your condition has worsened as you got into more socially demanding situations as an adult is important to your progression and control of the symptoms of the disorder.

In studies, high functioning individuals with autism (they studies kids between the ages of eight to fifteen) performed as well as adults in terms of basic language tasks but did not perform well when it came to complex language tasks like figurative language, Comprehension, Inference.

Individuals with high functioning autism or Asperger's are often extremely intelligent, displaying very good logical skills such as math or problem solving, however, their lack in social etiquette can halt them from progressing in a professional environment, this is why it is very important to begin to understand your condition as it stands now, what triggers the condition, how long you have displayed the symptoms and begin to put into place a plan which will enable you control or significantly improve your condition.

The stigma that used to lie within autism is no longer as prominent as more and more people begin to talk about their experiences with the condition.

Chapter 5 - Other Symptoms

There are also other traits that are not as obvious and are often caused by the triad symptoms.

For example, did you know that between 40% and 70% of people with autism suffer from sleep problems?

Often individuals with autism will develop indications that are independent of the diagnosis and since there is a tendency for autism to be connected with symptoms of other disorders.

There are a lot of signs that can develop. I want to go over the more common attributes that may pop up over the course of the disorder. Think back into your childhood and try to remember if some of these symptoms were apparent or whether you suffer from them now.

Sensory Abnormalities

Sensory abnormalities are the most common with 90% of those afflicted with autism experiencing some sort of sensory sensitivity. This could be things like being sensitive to light or overly distracted by noise, to the point where it effects concentration.

Some people with autism also have different sensory perceptions. For example, a soft touch may be painful for them or a firm grasp or a deep pressure can be calming for them. Some people have even reported not being able to feel pain.

Eating Habits

A correlating behavior has to do with eating habits.

Unusual eating behaviors are common as well. Selectivity is the most common problem.

While kids are often picky about what they eat, the severity of the case is what catches the attention of most professionals. Some kids will only eat one color of food. Others will only eat one type of food (such as oatmeal).

This type of behavior manifests as a phase that the kids do not grow out of. While it may be ritualistic, and while food refusal is a common problem, the children do not appear to be malnourished. Their eating habits often result in gastrointestinal issues.

In adults it can become a ritualistic way of eating rather than choice of food, so for example always eating vegetables before meat.

Motor Skills

Motor skills can also be affected. Some common traits include poor muscle tone, toe walking, and poor motor planning. Physical coordination is also pervasive. Like the other symptoms, these can seem like normal toddler and child behavior until the severity is considered.

Other comorbidities that are more specific to adults include (but are not limited to):

1) Cognitive problems with focus and concentration, and central coherence

2) Neurological and developmental issues (like ADHD, dyspraxia, and epilepsy)

3) Gastro-intestinal problems

4) Learning disabilities

5) Mental Health Issues

6) Sensory Problems

7) Functional and Adaptive Behaviors

8) Challenging and Disruptive behavior

9) Anger Management Issues

Chapter 6 - Management- What Can Be Done?

Getting an Official Diagnosis

In order for you to be officially diagnosed, you must see a clinician who specializes in adult autism. Diagnosing autism in adults can be difficult because most tests are designed for children. As such, the symptoms in children are much stronger than in adults. Despite this, a developmental pediatrician may be your best bet. If you have children in your family that have autism, contact the clinician that diagnosed that child. Even if he doesn't feel comfortable diagnosing an adult, he may be able to point you in the right direction or refer you to a specialist. If you are not sure who to contact first, try your usual doctor who should be able to point you in the right direction.

If you would like to do even more research about finding a specialist near you, contact a respected autism center in your region. Some great examples include the "Autism Speaks" Treatment Network.

You may be hesitant to reach out and see a doctor for fear of the diagnosis. However, getting a positive diagnosis can be a good thing. It gives you an explanation for some of the complications and problems that you've been experiencing your whole life. Getting this answer, though, is only the first step.

Management and Treatment

While there isn't a cure for autism, there are some great management techniques for the symptoms.

Various treatments are available for different levels of autism. The main goals of these treatments are to lessen the deficits that are normally caused by the disorder, to increase the quality of life, and to function independently.

It may be necessary to try various treatments in order to find one that best suits you. There is no one-size-fits-all treatment. In fact, the most effective interventions and treatments are caters specifically to each individual.

These are some of the courses of treatment a doctor would refer you for.

Alternative and Augmentative Communication:

These interventions are important since verbal and non-verbal communication deficiencies are at the core of autism. AAC treatments usually result in small gains but if you have high functioning autism such as Asperger's, this may be just what you need to help boost your communication skills.

Motor Sensory Interventions:

These types of interventions offer a wide range of formats and fields which are covered. Some examples of the various types include (but are not limited to):

1) Combined, multi-component

2) Touch

3) Smell and taste

4) Sight based

5) Manipulation

6) Physical Activity

7) Hearing

Assistive and Adaptive Technology:

This type of technology refers to products and devices that are used to help maintain functional capabilities of individuals. This can include mobile devices, online communities, robots, etc. If you have high functioning autism, chances are that you won't need these types of technologies. However, since it is always a case by case basis, don't rule them out just yet.

Psychotherapeutic Interventions:

This is a term that is used to describe a large range of therapies that are aimed at allowing and empowering people to be able to understand their abilities, difficulties, and motivations through various techniques with their therapist. Some examples include creative therapies (like music and art), psychodynamic (such as counseling), cognitive (like cognitive behavioral therapy) and interpersonal therapies (like groups meetings).

Behavioral and Developmental Interventions:

These types of interventions help encourage individuals to develop appropriate behavior and discourage inappropriate behavior. The severity of such behavior and the treatment can and will differ. Examples of these types of interventions include cognitive behavior therapy, intensive interaction, positive behavioral support, self-management, and any type of social skills group.

Residential Interventions:

These are designed to help improve home life and essential living skills. It doesn't just touch on home and living skills but also social skills and other life experiences. Some of these types of interventions include residential care, supported living, and sheltered housing. These types of programs are designed to help adults with autism get out on their own and lead semi or fully independent lives.

Dietary Interventions (supplements and diets):

These help to supplement your diet and can refer to pills capsules, liquids, or probiotics.

These various vitamins and supplements can help you if you have eating sensitivities and are not getting the appropriate amount of certain nutrients. Special diets can be formulated to help avoid, reduce, or encourage certain foodstuffs in order to improve your particular and current diet.

Extensive research has been done on what vitamins and minerals help improve cognitive abilities as well as other health factors. We will cover some supplements you can take at home in the home treatment section of the book.

Standard Health Care:

The purpose of this type of treatment is to help the individual maintain good health by giving them access to professionals like occupational therapists, speech and language therapists, and psychologists. Standard health care normally works in conjunction with other types of therapies such as behavioral, motor-sensory, and developmental interventions.

Educational Interventions:

These help individuals learn academic subjects and obtain the skills needed to gain cognitive skills or achieve qualifications.

Animal-Based Therapies:

These therapies include an animal, like a dog or a horse, to become a basic part of your treatment.

In fact, there have been quite a few positive reviews and feedback published about a therapy program assisted by dolphins that there is no "compelling scientific evidence" that the program did anything other than improve the subject's mood. While this type of therapy has been controversial (mainly because there is no scientific basis behind the results), it has proven to be effective in the past.

Employment Interventions:

These interventions are specific to helping adults with autism obtain or maintain long term employment.

Since the triad of symptoms can often impact social and communication aspects of a job, these interventions help individuals strengthen these skills so that they can successfully keep a job. Some of the different aspects of employment interventions include:

1)Practical advice

2) Vocational rehabilitation

3) Supported employment

4) Skill development (for "soft skills" like active listening, speaking, manners, problem-solving, planning, time management, communicating effectively, and teamwork)

5) Job development

6) Conflict resolution

7) Safety skills, and

8) Other areas which affect employment.

Rights-Based Interventions (Advocacy & Campaigning):

These interventions help individuals advocate for themselves and campaign for autism awareness. Sometimes, the act of being more educated about the disorder and advocating for its awareness is enough of an intervention to help you get through some road blocks that might be in your way.

Medications:

Pharmaceutical drugs can help with certain symptoms such as antidepressants, antipsychotics, anticonvulsants, and stimulants. Depending on your symptoms, there may be a medicine that can help you cope with specific traits. However, proper therapy and medications should always go hand in hand. Emergencies may turn up which make it necessary to implement coping strategies and other techniques that you can learn in therapy sessions instead of relying solely on pills.

Chapter 7 - Home Treatment

I want to emphasize the fact that there is no cure for autism.

That being said, there are many different types of therapies or techniques that can help you cope with the symptoms. I've listed a number of medical prescribed methods in the previous chapter. However, there are also many things you can do at home to help with your condition.

Some of you may feel as though you can actually best treat yourself or that you would like to try some home remedies before spending money with a professional. I must stress that although none of the techniques listed in this book can harm you, I would always always advise you get professional supervision and diagnosis before embarking upon any treatment plan.

Being an adult or a young adult with high functioning autism, you may already be living out on your own and you may already have a steady job. You may not, until now, taken the time to look into the subject of autism despite having a niggling feeling for years.

These home treatments are things you can try inexpensively at home to help alleviate the symptoms that cause you problems. Of course, any type of self-treatment or treatment in general, works best when you've got a great support team behind you.

Talk with your friends and family members. Tell them of your concerns and what you plan on doing in order to help yourself cope and manage the symptoms that you do observe.

Daily Routine

Anyone with autism or Asperger's will benefit from a daily routine. Not only does it maintain a comfortable schedule and ease anxiety, it gives you the opportunity to control the "disruptions" making them a little less scary to you.

For an example, if you have a set routine, but you know you have a social event with work coming up, you are able to move your own schedule around to accommodate it, which will alleviate the anxiety associated with the tasks you did have planned that day being disrupted.

A set guideline for rules and expectations can also help you at home or at work. If you've been having issues at home, have someone that you trust come in and show you how to perform certain tasks.

Have them write down some socially acceptable norms, so you can refer to the list before a situation is due to arise.

This especially works at your job too.

I suggest that you ask for a meeting with your boss in order for the both of you to discuss the specific rules and expectations that are needed of you. If you have a worker's manual, read it before your meeting and ask any questions that arise because of it.

Getting friends, family and colleagues on board with what you are trying to do is paramount, as it is much about getting others to understand how you may react or deal with situations as it is for you to learn to cope with your symptoms.

Verbal Cues and Training.

Many people with high functioning autism and Asperger's syndrome work best with verbal cues instead of non-verbal cues.

Talk with your friends, family, and coworkers and explain to them that you work best with verbal cues.

If you are in a romantic relationship, this can be especially important because the closeness that is required of an intimate couple is based on both verbal and non-verbal communication.

Explain to him or her that you don't mean to be rude or insensitive and that this is just how your brain works best: with verbal cues.

Helping others to understand how you communicate best is very important, as sometimes social cues are very difficult to pick up. You require people to be completely transparent with you.

A good example of this is sarcasm, autistic people often do not understand sarcasm or jokes, and take what people are saying very literally. This can cause embarrassing situations, so it is much better if your circle of people are educated in how you communicate best.

Knowledge

Knowing that you may have trouble understanding the "big picture" can help you figure out what kind of training/learning process works best for you. When you're trying to learn a new concept, try starting with part of a concept first and then add to it in order to slowly put the pieces together to form the big picture, instead of working with the big picture first.

Visual Supports

Visual supports are a great tool to help you learn, remember, and understand concepts, ideas, and activities. If you are having trouble remembering things or don't understand a concept, try writing it down or keeping a journal/schedule.

I have a planner that has big blocks of white paper for notes alongside the daily schedule. This would prove to be very useful for people who are autistic or who have Asperger's Syndrome.

Noise

If you have always found it hard to work at school, try looking around and finding the distracting noises in order to keep them to a minimum: fluorescent lighting (they hum like crazy), ticking clocks, loud neighbors, etc.

If you aren't able to quiet down the environment, try keeping a pair of headphones with you. Keep them plugged into something inconspicuous (like an mp3 player).

You don't have to turn it on. Just as long as the headphones can block out the outside noise, they should help. If that's a little too pricey for your needs, just try a pair of earplugs.

This is another occasion where friends and family can be supportive of you, so ensure you talk to them about noise being a distraction for you and let them know when you need to concentrate so they can try and keep the noise to a minimum.

Triggers

Sometimes, you may find that your symptoms worsen in certain situations. It is important that you start to keep a journal of these "triggers"

Doing so will help you either avoid these situations or better prepare for them, using some of the techniques listed below.

Coping Mechanisms for Stressful Situations

Stress is one of the biggest triggers for autism sufferers, and so is one of the most important things to try and control within your life.

One of the most difficult symptoms to deal with is anxiety, and this often comes from being uncomfortable in stressful situations.

Below are some basic tips on eliminating stress, but I have written a full chapter on it later in the book where I have discussed practical solutions to stressful situations.

Organize yourself to be more efficient and to minimize the number of surprises in your schedule.

Environmental Control

If you find that negative people cause you to be more stressed, start distancing yourself from them and try and surround yourself with people who you feel calm around.

This can also be said about objects, if certain objects distract you or cause disruptions and therefore anxiety, such as the phone ringing, then ensure you purchase a phone that has a silent mode.

Positive Feedback

Make sure you reward yourself for your successes and don't beat yourself up for your failures. If you manage a task that would normally cause anxiety without an issue, then reward yourself with something nice.

This is called positive re-enforcement, and subconsciously you will start to associate the handling of that task, with a positive feeling or reward and it should eventually start to become easier for you.

Leisure Activities

Rewarding yourself by planning some fun time during your weekends can really help motivate you to get through that tough spot during your work week.

Planning these activities in advance will also help you start and deal with your schedule changing on a regular basis as well as give you the opportunity to meet new people.

If this is a situation you would normally struggle with, then take someone with you, a familiar face who you feel generally calm with.

There are also groups designed for people with autism to meet each other and form relationships. You can usually find these online or on Facebook, so it's worth doing a little research to find out if any such events are held in your local area.

Exercise

Exercise is proven to lower stress levels due to the release of endorphins. The "Happy" hormone. So it goes without saying that exercise will help you deal with anxieties.

Obviously, exercise is not something you can do at the drop of a hat, for example, you may not be able to alleviate your stress at the moment it occurs if you are at work using this technique. However, just getting out and walking around the building, getting some fresh air, and taking a breather can help your mood and your stress level.

Try and make exercising for 20-30 minutes three times per week part of your regular routine. Not only will it give you a physical outlet for your frustrations, it will help you to meet new people and release stress reducing hormones.

Diet and Supplements

Eating healthy makes sure that your body is running on well and has a good amount of energy to burn. This can help alleviate fatigue and poor body function which can add to stress, causing triggers of symptoms.

There are also some supplements that can help you to not only be calmer generally but also supplements that help brain function.

A good quality Omega 3 supplement, is extremely helpful in maintain good brain function.

Hops are often a very good calming supplement, and you can even use things like lavender essential oils to help with the sleep issues that most autism sufferers have.

Before using any supplements, it is advisable you contact your doctor, particularly if you have any current medical conditions or take any medication.

Work Patterns

If you are at a job that has you sitting at a desk for long periods of time, get up and stretch every hour. Set an alarm to it.

Make sure your employer is aware of your situation and supports you with shifts that do not change regularly and a routine that supports your needs when at work.

Things like having the same lunch time every day can often be helpful. These are all things you can suggest to your boss at your meeting.

Breathing Exercises

Breathe in deep and slowly breathe out.

Let your mind relax.

Do this about five times to really help bring some oxygen into your system and to help you quickly calm down.

Patience

If you know that your next errand or task will require a bit of waiting, bring a book along with you so that your mind does not become anxious waiting.

Try not to be frustrated if the exercises are not working overnight. Much of suppressing the symptoms of autism involves practice and patience.

Body Awareness.

You might be stressed and not even realize it.

Look out for signs like insomnia, headaches, upset stomachs, lack of concentration, excessive tiredness, stress rashes and headaches.

If you are stressed, take a moment to find a coping mechanism that can work at that moment, utilize one of the suggestions above, or find something that works for you such as burning a candle, having a bath or reading a book.

Practice Makes Perfect.

 Work with someone that you trust.

Tell this person that you are anxious about this activity and that you would like his or her help to practice out your portion of the event and what to expect from any other participants.

This includes speeches, social gatherings (making small talk, meeting with clients or customers, etc.), Job interviews or every day activities like taking turns and putting yourself in other people's shoes.

Practice non-verbal communication with a trusted friend or family member.

Non-verbal communication can be difficult to understand for most people but those with autism find it especially problematic.

That doesn't mean that you can't pick up non-verbal cues if you practice.

Go through various, common scenarios. Print out pictures of what people do in various emotions and situations. Make flashcards for yourself.

There is no shame in practicing on your own if you make up visual tools like flashcards.

Google various emotions and try to find facial cues and try and learn these.

Have your friend or family member come up with "stock" phrases that you can use in various social situations. For example, what to say when:

1) You are first introduced to someone

2) You encounter a friend who is going through a sad time

3) You find yourself in a situation when you are feeling a certain emotion

4) You need to make small talk at a meeting

5) You don't understand what is going on around you

Role playing with someone you trust can be a very helpful tool, and you should never been afraid to ask these people for their support.

You can also practice your stock phrases in a mirror so that they become more natural to you and you don't become anxious about saying or remembering them.

Do walk-throughs with someone who is familiar with a new place when you have to change your schedule.

For example, if you find yourself at a new job that you have to travel alone to, have someone take you through the fastest or the most comfortable route for you. This will help to eliminate as much anxiety as possible.

With a little bit of planning and a lot of effort, you can find some great coping mechanisms or home treatments to help you get through some of the symptoms of autism.

If you've tried these and they don't seem to work for you, it might be time to go to use these methods alongside the medical interventions used in the previous chapter.

The first step, though, is to try and find what works for you, this will allow you to consult with your doctor about what you need the most help with.

Chapter 8 - Practical Strategies for Coping with Stress

Stress is normal.

It is part of everyday life and is a natural reaction that our body makes towards changes and pressures in our everyday life. Stress is the body's response towards external influences which generate a natural 'fight or flight' response. In this respect, people with autism is exactly the same as everybody else.

The main difference with autism sufferers is the way the stress is dealt with. Sometimes stress in autistic people can lead to further issues such as frustration, anger or depression.

Many things can influence and generate stress in normal everyday situations such as excessive noise, traffic, rude people and rapid changing environment. In fact, stress can be caused, to a greater or less degree, by almost anything in our environment.

The body usually responds to stress with this 'fight or flight' condition where the body's nervous and chemical balances are prepared to react to the stressful situation.

For example. Imagine the body's reaction if you were suddenly woken during the night by the sound of breaking glass on the street outside your home.

The body reacts swiftly towards this 'stressful' situation. You find that you become very awake suddenly. Your heart rate increases, as does your blood pressure. Your hearing and sight become extra sensitive as your body searches for more information. Your brain prepares you for the 'fight or flight' response. This is the natural way that your body responds to stress for survival.

If this response happens too often, or happens towards too many slight situations then this can have a detrimental effect on the body as a whole. Your heart, liver and kidneys work less efficiently, your immune system is less effective and you start to suffer from hypertension. Often you are more open to psychological problems and disorders.

It has been found that in many cases it is much harder to deal with and control stress in people with autism. An excess of sensory stimulations can overload the emotions and can magnify the problem.

Managing your stress levels and coping with stress uses many cognitive reasoning functions of the brain. Among these are recognizing the symptoms and feelings of stress, recognizing the causes for the stressful situation, developing a strategy which allows you to cope with stress, keeping full control of your emotions in an appropriate manner and managing all of these feelings at the same time.

Handling stress can be compared to juggling. If a person is given one ball to juggle then there is usually not a problem, even with two balls it is often fine. If a person is given three, four or five balls to juggle it becomes much harder to deal with juggling. Seeing the balls, catching the balls, throwing the balls. A sensory overload is inevitable.

An adult with autism will usually be able to cope with small amounts of stress – one or two balls – but when stress levels rise slightly, due to the environment around them, noise, talking, questions, disorientation etc, then stress levels rise too quickly for the person to cope with.

Understanding Stress

The first thing a person must do in order to manage stress levels is to identify and become aware of the causes of stress. Stress can be caused by many things but if you can identify the major causes within your life then the first step to managing stress has been taken.

Often people find it very helpful to keep a 'stress diary' for a few weeks, Try to record every case of stress, no matter how small, in the diary. Record the date, time, place, causes, reactions, feelings and how you dealt with it. What caused the stress, what eased the stress. How long it lasted. In fact, try to record every little detail, no matter how small. The diary will eventually be used to develop a coping strategy and patterns within each stressful situations may become apparent.

At the end of each day, look back on entries and try to assign each situation a brief summary.

Was the stress acute or mild. Was it controlled or could you not control it. If you did manage to control the situation how did you do so. Sometimes techniques such as deep breathing, removing yourself from the situation by walking away, or counting to ten, managed to control the stress. Record which techniques you used and how well they worked. What techniques did you use.

Was the stress important to your day or was it unimportant. Sometimes a stressful situation can occur which has very little importance to the person but the stress appears never the less. An example may be becoming agitated and stressed at seeing someone drop litter on the street rather than putting it into a bin. While little is obviously a problem, it is an unimportant situation to a person that could cause stress.

By recording every instance of stress in a diary like this you can remove yourself from the situation and stand back so that things become clearer. You can easily look back after a few weeks and take a calm objective view of each situation. You may find that you can see common triggers for stress, and common coping techniques. This is the aim of the diary and finding these triggers and coping strategies are often the first steps to handling stress in a more manageable way.

Managing stressful situations

There are commonly considered to be four major tools for managing stress. Each will develop a skill which can be used towards a coping strategy and each skill may be more useful it certain situations. The four skills that are usually used to control stress are

- Awareness of the stress levels and the situation.

- Accepting the situation and the developing stress

- Handling and coping with the stress and situation

- Behaviour and actions which positively affect the overall management of stress.

Awareness Skills

This is often the most difficult as it is the initial skill that identifies the stressful situation. Trying to generate a clearer understanding of the situation and how the situation is effecting the person involved. Becoming fully aware of the cause of the stress and the situation that the person is in is usually the hardest for a person to identify.

Acceptance Skills

Once the person had become aware of the situation and is aware of the stress and the effect it is having then the person should try to accept the situation. Try to take a realistic view on what is happening. How important is the situation that is triggering the stress. How easy is it for the person to control the stress. How important is the stress trigger. How important is the situation and thus the stress being caused.

Handling Skills

Being prepared to cope with a situation by using approaches that are familiar and useful to a person is often very difficult. By identifying the causes of the stress and assessing the importance and level of the stress allows a person to cope better. Being able to identify and control triggers of stress that are unimportant, by accepting that they are unimportant, is a good way of reducing the effect that the stress triggers can have on a person. Having a positive approach to known influences is always an ideal way of dealing with a situation. Realizing that the worries are less important and can easily be controlled by basic strategies often reduces the level of stress that is being caused.

Behaviour Skills

By having an active approach to the situation a person can often control their stress. Developing a few basic strategies that can be used to limit the stress and to help a person deal with the situation is the ultimate aim in stress management.

A Practical Example of Stress Management

Many of the points raised in the previous section are applicable to everyday life situations.

The example below uses a job interview to demonstrate how these skills can be applied to what would normally be a stressful situation.

Awareness skills:

Try to find out in advance what the interview will involve. Try to find out what you will be required to do. Often it is less stressful if things are known in advance.

How many people will be in the interview with you. Will you be required to demonstrate any skills or will it just be a question and answer session. How long is the interview expected to last.

These are basic things that will help you prepare for what you expect to be a stressful situation.

If you know what is expected then there should be less unknowns that can trigger stress levels.

Acceptance :

Recognizing the requirements for the interview allow you to accept the situation. You realize that the interview is important in order for you to get the job is the first step.

Knowing what is expected will help you accept that the interview will probably be tiring, you will be asked a series of questions. You may be needed to demonstrate a skill.

If you accept that you have very little control over the questions that will be asked and how long the interview will last you can start to control your thoughts and manage and cope with the situation in a much better way.

Handling skills:

Once you have become aware of the situation that is going to happen, and you have accepted that it needs to go ahead and what will be expected then you can start to develop a strategy to manage the stress.

Development of techniques such as talking through the situation to yourself beforehand is often a good way of coping. Developing a positive attitude towards the experience and accepting that it is a positive thing for you is always good.

Some people spend time before a situation such as this and practice how they are going to react.

There is nothing wrong with sitting in front of the mirror and talking about yourself as you would during the interview. You can physically see how you are acting, you are practicing the thinks you are going to say. You can try phrasing things differently without having the stress of the interview.

You are preparing yourself as well as you can so that the situation will be more familiar, so easier to handle, and so less stressful. Preparing for the interview by checking out the route, arriving in plenty of time and having everything with you that you need will all help you in coping with the situation.

You may choose to involve a friend or family member in this process and asking them for their opinions on your answers etc.

Behavior skills:

Now that you are fully aware of what to expect, you have accepted the situation and you have developed a few techniques to cope you need to actually go through with the interview.

Perhaps travel to the interview with a friend. Arrange time before the interview in a quiet relaxing place such as a park. Go back to the park to sit quietly and calming and relaxing afterwards. These are all things that you can do to help the situation.

You can control your actions and behavior so that the stress, which you know is inevitable, is reduced and managed.

You have assessed the full situation and taken every step possible to cope with the interview.

Exercises for Coping with Stress

By using the example of the interview we can demonstrate the four skills that can be used to control and manage stress. This is an ideal situation as we are aware of things before that happen and can make full preparations and accept the situation. There are times however, that a situation can trigger stress when it is not expected. A person would benefit from having developed a series of techniques which can be used to cope with these types of situation.

Muscle relaxing techniques.

Try to recognize the difference between relaxation and tension in muscles in different areas of the body. First of all, try to focus on the muscles in the arms and hands. These are often the first muscles to become tense in a stressful situation and are usually the easiest to relax.

Try to relax these muscles by tensing your hands into fists and tensing the muscles in the forearm. Hold your hands and arms tense for 5 seconds then slowly relax. Relax for 15 seconds before tensing your hands again.

Sometimes a soft rubber ball gripped in each hand helps to focus the tensing. Try to tense and relax like this for ten minutes a day for about three weeks.

This exercise will allow you to develop control over the tension in your hands and arms so that should you become tense due to a stressful situation you are better prepared to relax the tense muscles in your hands and arms.

The second area to try and focus on is the head and shoulders, including your face. Similar tense/relax techniques can be used on this area too. Slowly turn the head so that you are looking backwards over your left shoulder.

Try not to stretch too far though. Hold that position for five seconds then return your head to its normal forward facing position and relax for fifteen seconds. Do the same by turning your head to look over your right shoulder. Again, repeat this exercise for ten minutes a day for three weeks. Once again you are developing control over the tension in the muscles in this area.

The third area to focus on is the buttocks, legs and feet. Sit in a chair in an upright position with your feet flat on the floor. Keeping your heels on the floor, slowly and gently raise your toes so that the muscles in your legs become tense. Again, do not overdo this, this is an aid to relaxation and not a form of muscle workout. Hold your toes up for five seconds then relax back down for fifteen. Then do the same but lift your heels. Again for five seconds then relax for fifteen. The third action is to clench your buttocks for five seconds and then relax for fifteen. Trying these actions ten minutes each day for three weeks will help gain control of the tension caused by stress.

The final areas of muscles to consider are the chest stomach and lower back. By sitting in your chair upright you are already starting to ease tension in this muscle group. Allow your shoulders to relax and sink down, putting your chin on your chest. This causes you to slump slightly. Lift your chin up and pull your shoulders back. You should feel all of the muscles in your chest and lower back tense. Hold for five seconds and then relax for fifteen. Try this for ten minutes a day for three weeks.

All of these activities are aimed at helping you recognize tension in your body and help you to develop ways of reducing the tension at times of stress. Once you have managed to master these techniques you will find that you can better recognize tension in your body due to stress and manage to control it so that you are more relaxed and better equipped to deal with stressful situation

Breathing techniques.

Having a good sense of breathing techniques are vital to having a healthy mind and body. Most people do not think about how they breathe. It is a natural process of the body and no thought is needed.

The brain controls the breathing using a set of reflex action. That is the brain controls the breathing without any conscious input from the person. That doesn't mean that we have no control over out breathing. It just means that in everyday situations the body takes over the function of breathing and allows the person to focus on other matters around them.

For a person to develop a good breathing regime it is important that you understand your own current breathing techniques. The first aspect of breathing that you need to know is where you breathe from. Do you breath from your stomach or do you breathe mainly from your chest. Short rapid shallow breathes from the upper part of your chest always leads to tension and should be avoided if at all possible. The ideal breathing technique is to be breathing deeply and calmly through the nose. Controlled and relaxed breathing. Ideally you should feel more movement in the stomach area than in the chest area as you breathe in and out.

Try to set aside some time every day to practice your breathing. Find a quiet relaxed place and close your eyes. Breath in slowly, taking about five seconds to take the air in, hold for five seconds, then breathe out slowly for seven or eight seconds. Try to control how fast you breathe out. Breathe like this for ten minutes, one a day for two weeks. You should find that the whole exercise relaxes you and lowers stress. Especially if you can clear your mind while breathing. Learn this breathing technique so that you can apply this to times of stress where your breathing becomes rapid and shallow. Focusing on the deep breathing will also help to reduce stress levels.

The great thing about breathing techniques for stress relief is that you can do them anyway, so if you are experiencing stress at work, you can find a quiet place, perhaps in the lunch room or bathroom and use the technique to calm yourself down.

Imaginative Visualization.

A well established method of reducing and controlling stress is the use of imagination.

When stress is triggered we know how it effects us and if we can remove ourselves from the stress levels than we can cope much better. When you feel that stress is becoming too hard to handle, try and find a quiet spot away from the stress triggers and start up your imagination. Try to imagine a pleasant place, or remember nice things so that you can achieve a relaxed state of mind.

- Sit comfortably.

- Focus on the stress in the muscles of the body and use the techniques already covered to eliminate as much tension as you possibly can.

- Focus on deep slow relaxed breathing so that your heart rate and your blood pressure and reduced.

- Imagine that you are in a calm place, peaceful and tranquil with no stress triggers. This place can be imagined or somewhere you remember.

- Calmly make yourself aware that you are in control of the situation, convince yourself that you are letting the stress and tension flow out of your body.

Tell yourself 'I am letting go of stress, I am relaxing, I am in control'. Let this phrase be your mantra. Practice using these techniques for a few minutes twice a day for a few weeks until you become comfortable with it. It is one of the best ways of controlling the effects of stress. It is usually easiest to practice either early in the morning before the stresses of the day have taken hold, or last thing at night so that you are calm and relaxed and ready for sleep. After a couple of weeks practice you should find that you are able to use this technique each time you feel stress levels rising or you start to feel uptight and worried.

Evaluating for progress

No matter which of the strategies and techniques you use to control and cope with stress you should always try to find time afterwards to evaluate yourself.

At first this might seem like a difficult thing to do but after a while it becomes easier. It might help to focus on the following points.

- How did the stressful situation start, what triggers were involved. How did you realize what was happening. How severe was the level of stress.

- How did you rationalize the stress, how did you decide which strategy or technique to use.

- Which strategy or technique did you use, how easy was it to put into place and how effective were your actions.

- How did you let yourself back into the situation once you had control and were coping well.

- Did you need to use further strategies or techniques and if so which seemed to be the most effective.

Once you find the ability to evaluate each situation you will soon develop an understanding of the best techniques for each different situation.

Every person is different, and remember that everyone, to a greater or lesser extent, suffers from stress.

Stress, as we have explained, is a natural reaction of your body to triggers from the environment.

Learning how to control, minimize and thus cope with these bouts of stress is the way forward.

The better you can control the stressful situations the better you can deal with normal everyday happenings and the better you can deal with your autism.

Chapter 9 - Panic attacks and autism

Adults who are autistic are usually more prone to panic attacks, or anxiety attacks as they are sometimes called. Panic attacks are, to the sufferer, extremely terrifying.

The levels of stress and anxiety build up to such a level very quickly that the mind reacts as if it is in great danger in a situation that most people would not find worrying. Autism magnifies these situations and as such autistic adults are much more prone to panic attacks.

People of any age can suddenly start to suffer from panic attacks, not just adults with autism. A small minority of people will go on to develop panic disorder where the attacks become more severe and more frequent. These attacks can have a significant disruption to the standard of life of the sufferers.

These panic attacks can happen at any time, seemingly without any warning. Usually they only last for a few minutes but some severe panic attacks can last for up to an hour or more. Suffers usually find that between attacks they are worried and anxious about what caused the first attack and will there be another. This worry is often enough to cause a second, and sometimes more, attack.

Panic attacks are usually accompanied with other physical effects such as increased heart rate – sometimes heart palpitations – rapid uncontrolled breathing, sweating, muscle tension and sometimes muscle pain. The feeling of complete helplessness is often very overpowering.

Any person who suffers from these effects during a panic attack must realize that it is just the way the body reacts so stress triggers. The 'fight or flight' scenario again.

The brain triggers a boost in the release of adrenaline into the blood stream which in turn causes an increased heart rate and rapid breathing in order to supply the muscles with more oxygen in preparation for action.

The pupils may dilate to increase vision accuracy and this can cause dizziness and sometimes, in extreme cases, make the sufferer feel like the walls are closing in on them, thus increasing the stress levels. A vicious never ending circle of cause and effect. Even the imagination runs wild, sometimes imagining the worst possible scenario for the situation.

Panic attacks, when happening often, can often give rise to other problems. If a person has several panic attacks due to becoming stressed when using an elevator for example, then person will relate the panic attacks to the elevator and thus start avoiding elevators. This soon develops into a phobia where the thought of an elevator alone can bring on a panic attack. This can start having an impact on everyday living for some sufferers.

Treatment and dealing with panic attacks.

There are several well established treatments for panic attacks. Most people find that using a combination of a number of approaches works best. Most of the approaches that you, as a sufferer, can control have already been covered.

Try to identify the cause of the attack. Evaluate the severity of the trigger, how important is it, how controllable is it. Relax and remove yourself from the stress, find your happy place, control your breathing and your tension.

By using the methods already covered you will find that while the panic attacks are still happening, you can control the way you react to them. Try to take a controlled approach and you will find the ability to cope with the attacks becoming much easier.

Sometimes medication is used. Anti-anxiety drugs are often very strong and have a risk of side effects. Medication alone should not be used to deal with panic attacks. Counselling and a better understanding should always be used as well.

Exercise and diet have been considered to have an impact on panic attacks. A healthy body helps to generate an emotional state of well being. Regular exercise can sometimes help with the physical feeling of stress and tension.

Some foods such as caffeine or chocolate can trigger panic attacks as they can contain chemicals which can help to unbalance the equilibrium in the body and effect changes such as increasing heart rate. The increase in heart rate can sometimes trigger heart palpitations which will trigger a panic attack. Once again a circle of events that should be avoided.

Relaxation and meditation techniques have already been covered and the use of these techniques can, and will, help during panic attacks. Handling stress and controlling panic attacks, especially for adults with autism, are often very closely linked.

When you feel that a panic attack is developing the important thing to remember is to keep calm. As in controlling stress, evaluate and assess the causes, try to rationalize the triggers. Control your body and mind as best you can and try to use as many relaxation techniques as you can. Try to slow your heat rate, control your breathing and find a 'special place' in your mind in which to relax.

As with stress, try to evaluate the panic attack after it has finished. If you can understand the causes, and pinpoint the best techniques for controlling the attack you are well on the way to avoiding them. Or at least minimizing the effect that they will have on you. Try to face the causes of the panic attacks. Most causes are unpleasant but not dangerous. Try not to add unnecessary fear to an already difficult experience.

Most of all, try to remember. Anxiety, panic or stress cannot immediately hurt you. It might not be nice, and might not feel good, but you can control it.

Conclusion

I hope that from this book you have learnt a little more about the signs of Autism and how to cope with them, but more importantly, I hope you have learnt a little more about yourself.

I have seen many people work with their own strengths in order to live normally with Autism, and some of the techniques discussed in this book can really help improve those awkward social interactions that may otherwise seem daunting.

Remember, it is always important to seek the help of your doctor and talk through concerns rather than trying to self-diagnose, however, the methods in this book will help people both with Autism and with other disorders such as social anxiety disorder.

Finally, I want to wish you the best of luck in your journey and that you have success in controlling any symptoms that you may have.

Printed in Great Britain
by Amazon

28217147R00046